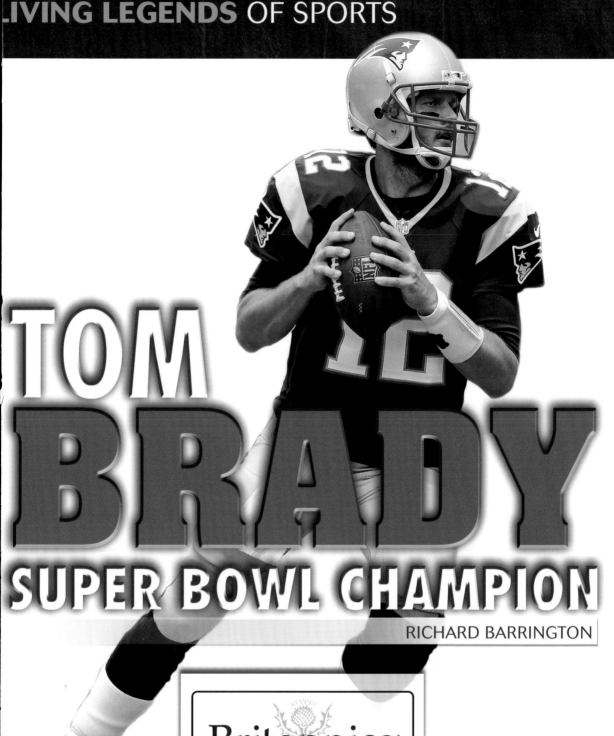

# TOM BRADY
## SUPER BOWL CHAMPION

RICHARD BARRINGTON

Britannica
Educational Publishing

IN ASSOCIATION WITH

ROSEN
EDUCATIONAL SERVICES

Published in 2016 by Britannica Educational Publishing (a trademark of Encyclopædia Britannica, Inc.) in association with The Rosen Publishing Group, Inc.

29 East 21st Street, New York, NY 10010

Distributed exclusively by Rosen Publishing.

To see additional Britannica Educational Publishing titles, go to rosenpublishing.com.

First Edition

**Britannica Educational Publishing**
J.E. Luebering: Director, Core Reference Group
Anthony L. Green: Editor, Compton's by Britannica

**Rosen Publishing**
Hope Lourie Killcoyne: Executive Editor
Nelson Sá: Art Director
Nicole Russo: Designer
Cindy Reiman: Photography Manager
Lucas Killcoyne: Expert Reviewer

Barrington, Richard, 1961–
Tom Brady: Super Bowl champion/Richard Barrington. -- First Edition.
        pages cm.—((Living Legends of Sports))
Includes bibliographical references and index.
ISBN 978-1-68048-119-8 (Library bound)—ISBN 978-1-68048-120-4 (Paperback)—ISBN 978-1-68048-122-8 (6-pack)
1. Brady, Tom, 1977––Juvenile literature. 2. Football players—United States—Biography—Juvenile literature. 3. New England Patriots (Football team)—Juvenile literature. I. Title.
GV939.B685B37 2015
796.332092—dc23
[B]
                                                                                                2014040287

*Manufactured in the United States of America*

# CONTENTS

# INTRO-
# DUCTION

Cameras flash and confetti flies through the air. Fans stay long after the football game to cheer the young quarterback of the New England Patriots as he lifts the Vince Lombardi Trophy for winning the Super Bowl. It is a night of firsts.

For that quarterback, Tom Brady, it is his first Super Bowl in his first season as starter. Because he played so well in the game, he will win his first Super Bowl Most Valuable Player (MVP) award. Even though his team, the Patriots, has been around for forty years, it is the team's first Super Bowl victory. All these firsts are just the beginning of a long run of success that Brady and the New England Patriots will have together. Yet it almost did not happen.

The Patriots very nearly did not win that game, and Brady was not supposed to be their starting quarterback. He might

The image of Tom Brady celebrating a Super Bowl victory became a familiar sight to American football fans over the course of his record-setting career.

not even have been drafted by a National Football League (NFL) team because he had trouble getting playing time in college. Come to think of it, his sports career could have gone in a very different direction because he started out playing baseball. One of the greatest careers in NFL history almost never happened.

This book is the story of how all the pieces fell into place to make that career possible. It is a story of beating the odds and continuing to try hard even when things go wrong. It is the story of how Tom Brady kept going, kept throwing, and kept surprising people.

# CHAPTER ONE

# An Unlikely Football Star

**T**om Brady grew up around sports in San Mateo, California, near the San Francisco Bay area. His parents, Tom Sr. and Galynn, took him to professional football and baseball games from an early age. His three older sisters were star softball players.

Born on August 3, 1977, Tom Jr. was four years old in 1981 when the local San Francisco 49ers played one of the greatest play-off games in NFL history. Tom's parents took him to that game, and the 49ers beat the Dallas Cowboys on a last-minute throw from Joe Montana to Dwight Clark. Many years later, Tom would be compared with Hall-of-Fame quarterback Montana.

Sports were a big part of Tom's early life. With his older sisters as an influence, Tom developed a competitive drive that would seem to mark him as a future athlete. There was just one problem: he did not always seem particularly athletic.

Joe Montana of the San Francisco 49ers—shown here in 1981 at the game young Tom Brady attended—was a four-time Super Bowl winner and Brady's boyhood idol.

# A Late Beginner

Young Tom was a slow runner, and early in high school he was a little overweight. The combination of those things led him initially to play

Though he found stardom in the National Football League, Brady was first drafted by a professional baseball team.

baseball instead of football. His position in baseball was one often given to players who cannot run very fast: catcher.

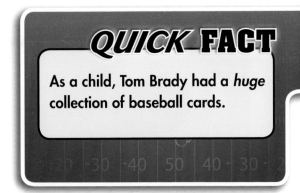

It was behind the plate that Tom first really blossomed as an athlete, becoming a good enough catcher to eventually be drafted by a Major League Baseball team, the Montreal Expos. Catchers help decide what pitches to throw the other team's batters, and this experience of studying the opposition and calling the plays would serve Tom well in the athletic role he really wanted: quarterback in football.

Tom did not make the varsity football team until his junior year at Junipero Serra High School, but once on the team he quickly became a starter. He established himself as a team leader because of his knowledge of the game as well as his commitment to putting in the effort it takes to get in top physical condition. He also worked on the way he threw, to get the most out of his talent.

The extra effort paid off. By the end of his senior year in high school, Tom was an All-State quarterback. He had also attracted the attention of several major colleges, including Big Ten Conference power Michigan.

# Fighting for Playing Time

When Tom Brady accepted a scholarship from Michigan, he expected to continue the success he had enjoyed as a high school quarterback. However, big schools such as Michigan have more than one player for each position, and each has to compete for playing time.

For Brady, this process was a slow one, and he did not play during his first year at Michigan. The next year, Brady was on the team but as a third-string quarterback who saw limited playing time. The year after that, Brady was a backup again and began to grow impatient. He complained

Brady played college football for the Michigan Wolverines of the Big Ten Conference.

to his coaches and threatened to transfer to another school. Then, he was sidelined by appendicitis. This medical condition, an inflammation of the appendix, sidetracked his season, but it turned out to be a blessing in disguise.

While recovering from emergency appendix surgery, Brady thought back to his high school career, remembering the importance of being a team player. He decided to be a leader instead of a complainer.

With his attitude straightened out, Brady was ready for the 1998 season, and finally he became the starter. He had a successful year, completing 62 percent of his passes with fourteen touchdowns, and led the team to a share of the Big Ten championship and a comeback victory in the Citrus Bowl.

THE HEISMAN MEMORIAL TROPHY
IS PRESENTED BY
DOWNTOWN ATHLETIC CLUB OF NEW YORK CITY
TO
RON DAYNE
UNIVERSITY OF WISCONSIN
AS THE
OUTSTANDING COLLEGE FOOTBALL PLAYER
IN THE UNITED STATES
FOR
1999

The performance of Heisman Trophy-winning quarterbacks after turning pro is a reminder that success in college does not guarantee success in the NFL.

Going into his senior season, it seemed that Brady had established himself as the team's starter and possibly a star in the making. However, the 1999 season began with Brady splitting time with Drew Henson, a player many felt was going to be a superstar. Once again, Brady would have to fight for playing time.

# College Quarterbacks and the NFL

Success at the position in college might seem to set the stage for someone to become a good NFL quarterback, but that is not always the case.

The Heisman Trophy is an award given annually to the best player in college football. Of the Heisman Trophy winners between 1963 and 2014, twenty-six were quarterbacks. Of these twenty-six, however, only five have gone on to long and reasonably successful pro careers. At this time, another six are still too young to determine how their careers will go. The remaining fifteen either turned out to mostly play backup, washed out after a short attempt at a pro career, or never even played in the NFL.

So, while playing quarterback in college can earn a player valuable experience and get the attention of NFL teams, it does not guarantee professional success. A college player drafted by an NFL team is back to where he was at the start of his college career: trying to make the cut and get in the game.

## *QUICK* FACT

As a college senior, Brady led Michigan to a 10–2 record, a share of the Big Ten championship, and a number five national ranking.

## A Grand Finale: The 2000 Orange Bowl

At the start of the 1999 season, Michigan head coach

Lloyd Carr decided that he would play both Henson and Brady at quarterback during games, switching back and forth between the two. Halfway through the season,

Though Brady's career at Michigan had its ups and downs, it ended in triumph with an Orange Bowl victory over Alabama.

though, he made the decision to go with Brady as the full-time starter. It proved to be a good call.

Michigan won ten games with just two losses, and the team was selected to play in the Orange Bowl after the regular season. On January 1, 2000, Michigan squared off against Alabama, which quickly jumped out to a 14–0 lead. Brady was even benched briefly, in favor of Henson. With Brady back in the game, Michigan scored two touchdowns to tie the game up at 14-all. Once again, though, Alabama got the upper hand, scoring the next two touchdowns to lead 28–14. It was midway through the third quarter, and time was running out on Brady's college career.

## QUICK FACT

In helping his team win a comeback victory in the Orange Bowl, Brady set Michigan and Orange Bowl records for passing.

Late in the third quarter, Brady led Michigan to two touchdowns within five minutes to re-tie the game at 28-all. The fourth quarter was scoreless when Brady and the Michigan offense took over with less than three minutes left. Brady led his team inside the 20-yard line, within range for an easy field goal that would give them a dramatic, come-from-behind victory—except the kick was blocked!

If he had not already had to fight through so many struggles in his career, Brady might have been rattled by that setback. Instead, he kept fighting and led his team to a 35–34 overtime victory. When it was over, Brady had thrown four touchdown passes and set Michigan and Orange Bowl passing records. It was a perfect ending to a college career and seemed to set him up well for the next phase of his career: the NFL.

# From the Bench to Champion

**I**t might seem as though Brady's great game in the 2000 Orange Bowl was the breakthrough that launched him to NFL success, but it did not happen that way. A few months later, when NFL teams gathered to select college players through the draft, it looked as though Brady had been forgotten. It was not until the sixth round—the next-to-last round of the draft—that the New England Patriots chose Brady.

Getting drafted into the NFL does not mean that a player will automatically make the team—especially for low-round picks such as Brady. He had some work to do. He was considered slow and did not have the type of cannon for an arm that NFL scouts favor. Although at 6'4" he was a good height for an NFL quarterback, his body was underdevel-

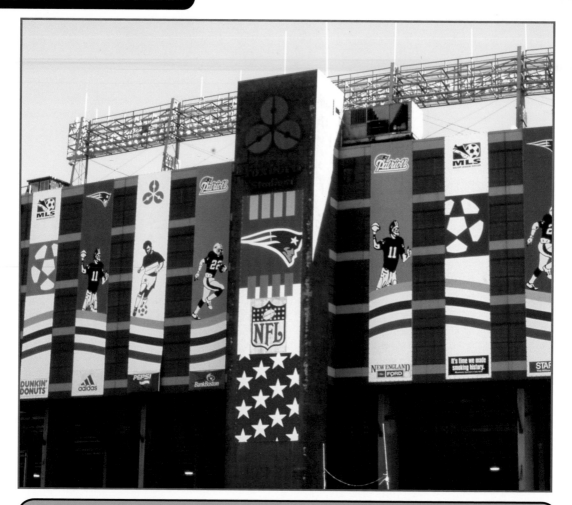

Despite not being drafted until the sixth round, Brady would go on to find stardom playing for the Patriots in New England.

The task ahead was clear: Brady would have to build himself up physically, while also learning the complex playbook of the Patriots. After starting from the bench and working his way into a starting and then starring role in college, Brady would have to repeat the process in the pros.

# Late-Round Steals

Before the NFL's yearly draft, there is a great deal of speculation about who the number one pick will be. That top pick is rewarded with a big contract, instant fame, and usually a starting job.

For lower-round picks it is a different story. Many are selected just to fill out the numbers, and some will never make an NFL team. Now and then, though, one of these low-round picks rises to become a star. These are called late-round steals, because the team gets much more than it bargained for with a low draft pick.

Brady was picked in the sixth round of the 2000 draft. Other great players drafted in the sixth round or later include Pro Football Hall-of-Famers Richard Dent, Ken Houston, Shannon Sharpe, and Rayfield Wright.

# Playing Behind an Established Star

Being a late-round pick was not Tom Brady's only problem. The Patriots already had an established star quarterback in Drew Bledsoe, who had led the team to the Super Bowl a few years earlier.

Another problem was that the Patriots were not very good, winning just five games against eleven losses in Brady's first season. Brady tried to remain patient and focus on things he could control, such as learning more about how plays were called and adding some muscle to his skinny frame.

When he arrived in New England, Brady was originally a little-used backup to established starter Drew Bledsoe, pictured here avoiding a Colts pass rusher.

He played in just one game during his rookie season, completing one pass for six yards.

# A Dramatic Entrance

The 2001 NFL season began with Bledsoe still as the Patriots' starter and Brady on the bench. There was a difference this year, however. In the off-season, Brady had added fifteen pounds of muscle. This weight gain gave him a bigger frame better suited to the pounding of NFL tacklers, and the extra strength also added some oomph to his passes. All in all, Brady went into his second season more ready to be a professional quarterback.

That readiness soon paid off. In just the second game of the season, Bledsoe was chased toward the sidelines and hit hard in the chest by New York Jets linebacker Mo Lewis as Bledsoe went out of bounds. He tried to continue, but the injury was serious. As Bledsoe headed out of the game and toward the hospital with a damaged blood vessel, Brady became the team's starter.

Early in Brady's second season, he got a chance to shine as New England's starter after an injury to Bledsoe.

Brady had his ups and downs at first, but as the season went on, things really started to click. The Patriots won their last six games to finish 11–5 and make the play-offs. Meanwhile, even though Bledsoe had recovered from his injury, Patriots coach Bill Belichick made the decision to stick with Brady as the starter.

## QUICK FACT

Brady played in just one game and completed just one pass in his rookie season.

# Super Bowl XXXVI: A Night of Firsts

Brady showed a flair for the dramatic in his first play-off game. With the Patriots trailing the Oakland Raiders by 10–0 in the fourth quarter on a snowy evening in New England, Brady led the Patriots back to tie the game at the end of regulation and then win it in overtime. The Patriots then beat the Pittsburgh Steelers the following week; they were on their way to the Super Bowl.

Even after Bledsoe's return from injury, Patriots' coach Bill Belichick decided to stay with Brady as his starter.

The only problem was that Brady had badly injured his ankle in the Pittsburgh game, and Bledsoe had come off the bench to lead the team to victory. In the week leading up to the Super Bowl, the press and fans debated and speculated about who should be the starter. One man's mind was made up, though. Coach Belichick was convinced that his team ran better with Brady at quarterback. Once Brady's ankle was healthy enough to play on, he named Brady the starter.

The Patriots went into the Super Bowl as huge underdogs against the St. Louis Rams. It was a close game, though, and when the Patriots got the ball at their 17 yard line with one minute and twenty-one seconds left, the game was tied 17–17. With the end zone more than 80 yards away, it looked as though the game was headed for overtime.

Brady and his teammates, however, had other ideas. They drove down to the 30-yard line, but with seven seconds left, there was no real

With some clutch help from kicker Adam Vinatieri, Brady led the Patriots to victory in Super Bowl XXXVI.

choice but to try for a field goal. It would be a long one, but as time ran out, kicker Adam Vinatieri nailed it to give the Patriots the victory.

For the Patriots, it was their first Super Bowl victory in three tries. For Tom Brady, it was total success in his first season as starter, and he was named the game's MVP. It was a night of firsts, and it was only the beginning.

# Building on Success

**T**hey say that the only thing harder than winning a championship is defending a championship. The Patriots found that out first-hand when they were eliminated from play-off contention in the final week of the 2002 season, less than a year after winning the Super Bowl.

Tom Brady threw twenty-eight touchdowns, but like the rest of his team, he struggled toward the end of the season. When it was over, there was nothing they could do but watch the play-offs on television and start thinking about the next season.

## Three Rings in Four Years

As is the case with many champions, Tom Brady and the Patriots dealt with disappointment by stepping up their effort and determination. It paid off in the 2003 season as the Patriots earned a play-off spot and fought their way back to the Super Bowl in early 2004.

Two seasons after their first Super Bowl victory, Brady and the Patriots became champions again by beating the Carolina Panthers in Super Bowl XXXVIII.

Super Bowl XXXVIII was a strange game. It took almost all of the first half before there was any score at all—the longest any Super Bowl had gone with no points. Then, in the fourth quarter, the floodgates opened. The Patriots and their opponents, the Carolina Panthers, combined for 37 points in the final period, a Super Bowl record for the most total scoring in the fourth quarter.

With just seconds left and the score tied at 29, kicker Vinatieri, a play-off hero for the Patriots two seasons earlier, lined up to attempt a

## QUICK FACT

Tom Brady was named MVP in his first two Super Bowls. In 2015, eleven years after his second MVP award, Brady led the Patriots to the NFL championship once again, earning his third such award.

In addition to getting a second championship ring, Brady earned his second MVP award for Super Bowl XXXVIII.

41-yard field goal. Earlier in the game, Vinatieri had missed a shorter field goal and had seen another attempt blocked. However, he ignored those failures and hit the field goal with four seconds to spare. The Patriots won 32–29.

That last-second drama would not have been possible without the efforts of Brady, who passed for 354 yards and three touchdowns. For the second time in three years, he was named Super Bowl MVP.

The Patriots accomplished the difficult feat of repeating as champions when they defeated the Philadelphia Eagles in the Super Bowl the following year. It was another close game, with the Patriots winning 24–21. The Patriots became one of just eight teams to win back-to-back NFL champion-ships, and the Patriots and the Dallas Cowboys of the mid-1990s became the only NFL teams to win three rings in four years.

What was more important than the history was that the Patriots were a successful team with a young quarterback at the helm. They looked like a dynasty that would continue for years.

> ## QUICK FACT
>
> The Patriots won Super Bowls after the 2003 and 2004 seasons, giving them three championships in four years. After a long dry spell, they came back again in Super Bowl XLIX, in 2015.

## An Almost-Perfect Season

Though the Patriots won their division in each of the next two years, they failed to make the Super Bowl. During the 2007 season, though, it looked as though nothing could stop them. The Patriots went 16–0 during the regular season and rolled through two play-off wins to make it to Super Bowl XLII against the New York Giants.

The Patriots were heavily favored to complete their season by becoming the first 19–0 team in NFL history. They led until late in

An upset win by Eli Manning and the New York Giants in the 2008 Super Bowl ended a bid for a perfect season by Brady and the Patriots.

the fourth quarter when Giants quarterback Eli Manning brought his team downfield for a wild comeback touchdown. The Giants won 17–14.

Manning and the Giants frustrated the Patriots again following the 2011 season. The teams met in Super Bowl XLVI, and the two quarterbacks staged a classic duel. Once again, though, Manning led a last-minute touchdown drive to defeat the Patriots. This time, the Giants won 21–17.

# The Patriots: Winning and Losing the Big Game

With six Super Bowl appearances having Brady as quarterback along with two showings prior to his joining the team, the Patriots have a prominent place in Super Bowl history—for better or worse.

As of the 2015 Super Bowl only two teams, the Cowboys and the Steelers, have also appeared in eight Super Bowls. The bad news is that only one team, the Broncos, have lost more (five). To date, the Patriots are one of four teams to have four Super Bowl losses.

When it happens, losing a Super Bowl can look like a big disappointment. However, to the thirty teams each year that do not get to the Super Bowl, just making it to the big game seems like a pretty successful season.

Following that third Super Bowl victory back in February of 2005, the Patriots won their division in nine of the next ten years, returning to the championship game three times.

## Brady and the Mannings

While it was Eli Manning who twice stood in the way of Brady winning another Super Bowl, it was another Manning—Eli's brother Peyton—whose career most often seemed closely tied to Brady's; he and Peyton Manning were most often compared as the top quarterbacks of their time. The two had some memorable duels on the field and played tug-of-war with the record for most touchdown passes in a season. Manning set a record in 2004 when he threw forty-nine touchdown passes, but Brady topped him in 2007 with fifty. Not to be outdone, Manning took the record back with fifty-five in 2013.

Even as Manning set that record in 2013, Brady still had the

A championship ring is highly coveted by NFL players because it is the ultimate symbol of team success.

## QUICK FACT

Tom Brady set a record with fifty touchdown passes in 2007 though it was later broken when Peyton Manning threw fifty-five in 2013.

upper hand in one key respect. As both of their careers entered their final years, Brady had four Super Bowl rings, while Manning had just one.

## 2015: "DeflateGate"

Following the 2014 regular season, Brady helped the Patriots get over its hump as New England routed the Indianapolis Colts in the

As the most successful quarterbacks of their era, Brady and Peyton Manning were often compared to one another.

AFC championship, earning Brady his record sixth Super Bowl start. However, that victory was soon awash in controversy, as it was alleged that eleven of the twelve footballs that the Patriots had used in the game were underinflated, which can make them easier to grip and travel farther when thrown.

The NFL looked into the incident but no action was taken before Super Bowl XLIX, where Brady led a fourth-quarter rally in a 28–24 win over the Seattle Seahawks. Brady passed for 328 yards and four touchdowns in the contest to earn his third Super Bowl MVP trophy.

Following an independent investigation whose findings were released in May 2015, Brady was found to have been "at least generally aware" of plans by Patriots personnel to deflate the game balls. As a result, he was to be suspended for the first four games of the 2015 season. The Patriots were fined $1 million and lost a couple of draft picks, including a first rounder.

# CHAPTER FOUR

# On and Off the Field

**B**eing a Super Bowl-winning quarterback would be enough of a dream come true for most sports fans, but Brady has more going for him than success on the field. With his all-American good looks, Brady has become a celebrity whose fame goes beyond the world of sports.

Brady was named one of *People* magazine's 50 Most Beautiful People in 2002, and some of the world's loveliest women have taken notice. He had a long-term relationship

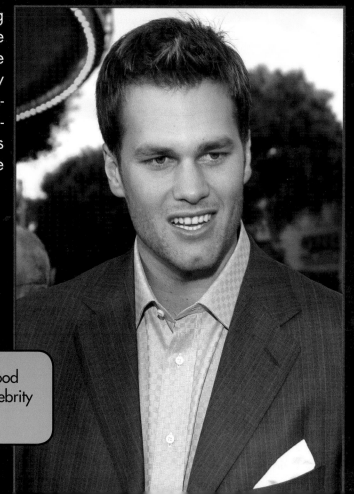

Brady's on-field success and his good looks have helped make him a celebrity and a sought-after endorser.

with actress Bridget Moynahan, and the two had a son named John together in 2007, though they had already broken up by the time the baby was born. Brady married supermodel Gisele Bündchen in 2009,

Brady has been married to supermodel Gisele Bündchen since 2009.

and the couple has two children together, a boy named Benjamin and a girl named Vivian.

# Private Life and Public Image

With his athletic success and celebrity relationships, Brady is very much in the public eye, yet he does not actively seek attention. He described his focus to *People* magazine in this way: "I prioritized with the things that are important to me . . . That's my family and my football career. There's nothing other than that."

In a similar way, Brady has earned his share of commercial sponsorships but has managed to remain low-key about it. He tends to endorse luxury brands and usually in print ads rather than extensive television campaigns. So, while he is in the public eye, he has not made himself into a global brand as has Michael Jordan, nor developed a well-known public personality such as Peyton Manning has done.

*QUICK* **FACT**

Brady and Bündchen have two children together: Benjamin Rein and Vivian Lake.

In short, for someone with four Super Bowl rings, a supermodel wife, and various celebrity endorsements, Brady has been able to keep his personal thoughts and feelings unusually private.

# Where Brady Stacks Up with History's Greats

As is the case with many sports, professional football has a Hall of Fame to help fans remember great players from the past. Decade after decade, there have been star players at the quarterback position who were later elected to that Hall of Fame. Johnny Unitas, Joe Montana, and Dan

Former Dolphin quarterback Dan Marino is among those players often included with Brady in a discussion of who is the NFL's all-time greatest.

Marino are just a few stars from the past who are considered among the best to ever play the quarterback position.

Does Tom Brady belong on that list? It seems clear that he does. As he entered the later years of his career, he had already climbed into the all-time top-five in career wins and career passing touchdowns. Earlier in his career he had set records for most regular season wins in a row, with twenty-one, and for most play-off games won in a row, with ten.

Add to that four Super Bowl rings and three Super Bowl MVP trophies, and it is clear that Tom Brady has achieved the individual

The 2014 season saw Brady and the Patriots return to the play-offs and to Super Bowl success.

and team success necessary to be considered among the very best quarterbacks of all time.

In fact, following the 2015 Super Bowl, the NFL itself—on its official website—wondered: "Is Tom Brady the greatest quarterback of all time?" Here's the text:

*Tom Brady just won his fourth Super Bowl (equaling Joe Montana and Terry Bradshaw for the most ever by a quarterback) and third Super Bowl MVP (matching Montana for the most by any player). Not to mention, Brady just passed Montana for most career touchdown passes in the Super Bowl (13) and Peyton Manning for most completions in a single title game (37).*

In a postgame interview with NFL Network's Alex Flanagan, Julian Edelman couldn't help but be in awe of his highly decorated teammate:

*He's the greatest quarterback ever to live on this Earth. He's won four Super Bowls in the modern-day era with a salary cap. He's been to six. I'm a huge Joe Montana fan, I love him to death, but Tommy's No. 1.*

Brady is beloved by New England fans and respected throughout the NFL.

# The Difficulty of Comparing Players Across Eras

When people talk about great quarterbacks, the discussion often comes down to trying to figure out who was the greatest quarterback of all time. People like to use statistics to try to answer these questions, but the numbers do not tell the whole story. First of all, which statistic is more important: touchdowns or wins? Completion percentage or total yardage? The fact is that quarterbacks shine in various areas of the game, so different statistics tell different stories about how great they were.

Also, the game has changed over time. Before the 1970s, few games were played in domes or on artificial turf, so quarterbacks more often had to deal with wind and slippery turf. Seasons used to be shorter, too: a quarterback could not be expected to throw as many touchdowns in a fourteen-game season as one who played sixteen regular-season games. The size of players—on both offense and defense—have changed over time as well, making throwing a pass in 1965 a very different thing from throwing one in 2016.

Finally, the other difficulty in comparing quarterbacks from different times—or even from the same era—is that football is a team game. Each quarterback has different receivers to throw to and different offensive lines blocking for them. Each is called upon to do different things by his coach.

So there is no perfect way of answering the question of who is the greatest quarterback of all time. The only sure thing is that in the future, Tom Brady will absolutely be one of the names in the thick of that discussion.

# A Team Player

After a long and successful career, how will Brady be remembered? Will it be for his individual passing record and his Super Bowl MVP trophies? Will it be because of his celebrity status and supermodel wife? Will it have to do with his personal story of overcoming doubters to achieve stardom?

Certainly, all of these things and more will be part of the legend of Tom Brady. If he had a choice, though, there is one thing for which he most likely would want to be remembered: "Winning games is the most important thing," he told the *Boston Globe* in 2014. "Whatever matters to you as an individual, it's far distant from what the team goals are. And the team goal is one thing: to score more points than the other team."

Winning is indeed the point of the game. When the regular season wins, play-off victories, and NFL championships are added up at the end of Brady's career, there is no doubt that he will indeed be remembered as a winner.

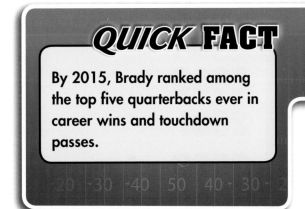

## QUICK FACT

By 2015, Brady ranked among the top five quarterbacks ever in career wins and touchdown passes.

# TIMELINE

**August 3, 1977** Tom Brady is born in San Mateo, California.

**1993** Brady becomes varsity quarterback as a junior at Junipero Serra High School.

**1995** Graduates high school and enrolls at the University of Michigan.

**1998** Brady is named the starting quarterback at Michigan.

**2000** Brady leads Michigan to Orange Bowl victory in his final college game.

**2000** Brady is drafted by the New England Patriots in the sixth round.

**2001** Brady takes over as starter after quarterback Drew Bledsoe is injured.

**2002** Brady is named Super Bowl MVP as New England wins NFL championship.

**2004** Brady is again named MVP as New England wins its second championship.

**2005** Brady quarterbacks the Patriots to their third Super Bowl win in four years.

**2007** Brady leads the Patriots to an undefeated regular season.

**2009** Brady marries supermodel Gisele Bündchen.

**2015** Brady is once again named MVP as New England wins the Super Bowl.

**Joe Montana (1956–)** One of the most successful quarterbacks in NFL history, Montana led the San Francisco 49ers to four NFL championships from 1982 to 1990 and was named Super Bowl MVP three times.

**Emmitt Smith (1969–)** As a member of the Dallas Cowboys, running back Emmitt Smith helped his team win three Super Bowls during the 1990s. When he retired after the 2004 season, Smith was the NFL career leader in rushing yards and rushing touchdowns.

**Michael Strahan (1971–)** One of the best pass rushers in NFL history, defensive end Michael Strahan set the NFL single-season record for quarterback sacks with 22½ in 2001. His New York Giants team defeated the New England Patriots in the 2008 Super Bowl.

**Peyton Manning (1976–)** A former first overall pick in the NFL draft, quarterback Manning led the Indianapolis Colts to a Super Bowl championship in 2007. Then, after overcoming a career-threatening injury, he joined the Denver Broncos and led them to a Super Bowl appearance in 2014.

**Calvin Johnson (1985–)** The wide receiver popularly known as "Megatron" is a favorite of sports highlights shows for his spectacular catches. He averaged over 1,000 yards and nearly ten touchdowns a season in his first seven years in the NFL.

# GLOSSARY

**backup**  A person or thing that serves as a substitute and can be used to replace or support another person or thing.

**celebrity**  Someone who is famous or celebrated.

**draft**  A system whereby exclusive rights to selected new players are apportioned among professional teams.

**end zone**  An area at the end of each football field, extending ten yards deep, that players have to reach in order to score a touchdown.

**field goal**  A score of three points in football made by drop-kicking or place-kicking the ball over the crossbar from ordinary play. (Drop-kicking is, however, a rather unusual course of action in the game.)

**Hall of Fame**  A group of individuals in a particular category (such as a sport) who have been selected as particularly illustrious.

**linebacker**  A football player on the defending team whose usual position is a short distance in back of the line of scrimmage.

**overtime**  Extra time that is added to a game when the score is tied at the end of the normal playing time.

**play-offs**  A tournament played by the leading regular season teams to see who wins the league championship.

**quarter**  One of four periods of fifteen minutes apiece that comprise the regulation time of a football game.

**quarterback**  A football player who leads his team's attempts to score, usually by passing the ball to other players.

**regulation**  The normal playing time of a game, not counting overtime. In professional and college football, one-hour games are divided into four periods of fifteen minutes each.

**scholarship**  An amount of money that is given by a school, an organization, a group, or an individual to a student to help (or completely) pay for a student's education.

**starter** A player on a team who begins the game at a given position and typically plays most of the time at that position because he or she is considered to be the best performer available on the team.

**Super Bowl** The annual championship game of the National Football League.

**touchdown** A score in football that is made by carrying the ball over the opponent's goal line or by catching the ball while standing in the end zone.

**underdog** A person or team expected to lose a contest or battle.

**varsity** The main team of a college, school, or club in a particular sport.

**Vince Lombardi Trophy** The prize awarded for winning the Super Bowl, named after a legendary Green Bay Packers coach who won the first two Super Bowls. Lombardi famously said, "Winning isn't everything, it's the only thing."

# FOR MORE INFORMATION

## Books

Berman, Len. *The Greatest Moments in Sports.* Naperville, IL: Sourcebooks Jabberwocky 2012.

Garner, Joe and Bob Costas. *100 Yards of Glory: The Greatest Moments in NFL History.* New York, NY: Houghton Mifflin Harcourt 2011.

Layden, Tim. *Sports Illustrated NFL Quarterback [QB]: The Greatest Position in Sports.* New York, NY: Sports Illustrated, 2014.

Lupica, Mike. *Game Changers* (Book 1). Bayside, NY: Scholastic Press, 2012.

Price, Christopher. *New England Patriots New & Updated Edition: The Complete Illustrated History.* Minneapolis, MN: MVP Books, 2013.

Savage, Jeff. *Tom Brady* (Amazing Athletes). Minneapolis, MN: MVP Books, 2014.

*Sports Illustrated* editors. *Big Book of Who: Football.* New York, NY: Sports Illustrated, 2013.

## Websites

Because of the changing nature of Internet links, Rosen Publishing has developed an online list of websites related to the subject of this book. This site is updated regularly. Please use this link to access this list:

http://www.rosenlinks.com/LLS/Brady